Pupil Book 2

Spelling

Skills

Author: Sarah Snashall

HarperCollins PUBLISHERS

Since 1817

William Collins' dream of knowledge for all began with the publication of his first book in 1819.

A self-educated mill worker, he not only enriched millions of lives, but also founded a flourishing publishing house. Today, staying true to this spirit, Collins books are packed with inspiration, innovation and practical expertise. They place you at the centre of a world of possibility and give you exactly what you need to explore it.

Collins. Freedom to teach.

Published by Collins
An imprint of HarperCollins*Publishers*
The News Building
1 London Bridge Street
London
SE1 9GF

Browse the complete Collins catalogue at
www.collins.co.uk

Publishing Director: Lee Newman
Publishing Manager: Helen Doran
Senior Editor: Hannah Dove
Project Manager: Emily Hooton
Author: Sarah Snashall
Development Editor: Jessica Marshall
Copy-editor: Tanya Solomons
Proofreader: Gaynor Spry
Cover design and artwork: Amparo Barrera
and Ken Vail Graphic Design
Internal design concept: Amparo Barrera
Typesetter: Jouve India Private Ltd
Illustrations: Beatriz Castro, Caroline Romanet, Jacqui
Davis, Eva Morales, Adrian Bijloo, Aptara and QBS
Production Controller: Rachel Weaver

Printed and bound by Martins the Printers

MIX
Paper from
responsible sources
FSC™ C007454
www.fsc.org

This book is produced from independently certified FSC paper to ensure responsible forest management.

For more information visit:
www.harpercollins.co.uk/green

Contents

Words ending in –ge

The **/j/** sound at the end of a word can be spelt **–ge**.

- a**ge**
- pa**ge**

Get started

Copy the words and underline the **/j/** sound. One has been done for you.

1. page

    Answer: pa<u>ge</u>

2. rage

3. strange

4. range

5. cage

6. large

7. barge

Try these

Look at the pairs of words. Copy the word with the correct spelling in each pair. One has been done for you.

1. wage, waje

  Answer: *wage*

2. bulj, bulge

3. change, chanje

4. charge, charje

5. message, messaje

Now try these

Find the spelling mistake in each sentence. Then rewrite the sentences with the correct spelling. Underline the correct spelling. One has been done for you.

1. My grandfather's aje is 72.

  Answer: *My grandfather's <u>age</u> is 72.*

2. She lives in a small cottaje by the sea.

3. Ed likes to sing on the staje.

4. The clown's shoes are huje.

5. I like to drink oranje juice.

Words ending in –dge

If a **/j/** sound comes at the end of a word after a short vowel sound, we often use **–dge**.

- ba**dge**

- e**dge**

Get started

Look at the groups of words. Copy the word in each group that ends in **–dge**. One has been done for you.

1. plod, splodge, soggy

   Answer: splodge

2. log, lodge, large

3. nudge, rude, huge

4. jug, jiggle, judge

5. sledge, sage, singe

6. fudge, fog, feud

7. egg, end, edge

Try these

Look at the pictures and write the words. One has been done for you.

 **1.** s _ _ _ _ _

Answer: smudge

 **2.** f _ _ _ _

 **3.** b _ _ _ _ _

 **4.** f _ _ _ _ _

Now try these

Find the spelling mistake in each sentence. Then rewrite the sentences with the correct spelling. Underline the correct spelling. One has been done for you.

1. My birthday bage has balloons on it.

Answer: My birthday <u>badge</u> has balloons on it.

2. I lost my ball in the hege.

3. There is orange jelly in the frige.

4. Under the brige lives a jolly old troll.

5. The slimy slug is covered in sluge.

Spelling c before e, i and y

The **/s/** sound is spelt **c** if it is before **e**, **i** or **y**.

- **c**eiling

- a**c**id

- i**c**y

Get started

Look at the groups of words. Then copy the word or words in each group where the **c** stands for a **/s/** sound. Underline the letter that follows the **c**. One has been done for you.

1. city, sit, duck

   Answer: c<u>i</u>ty

2. spice, spike, nice

3. pen, pencil, fossil

4. cell, sell, call

5. cycle, style, recycle

Try these

Look at the pictures and write the words. One has been done for you.

1. a blue c _ _ _ _ _

Answer: circle

2.  a s_ _ _ _ of pizza

3. a glass of orange j _ _ _ _

4.  a girl's f _ _ _

5. a bowl of breakfast c _ _ _ _ _

Now try these

Copy the sentences and underline **c** when it stands for the **/s/** sound. One has been done for you.

1. I celebrate my birthday once a year.

Answer: I c̲elebrate my birthday onc̲e a year.

2. At the circus we saw some silly clowns.

3. We saw the cricket ball sail over the fence.

4. Your lacy dress is very fancy.

5. Lemons and limes are citrus fruits.

Words beginning with kn– and gn–

When a word begins with **kn–**, the **k** is silent and the sound is **/n/**.

- **kn**eel

When a word begins with **gn–**, the **g** is silent and the sound is also **/n/**.

- **gn**at

Get started

Copy and complete the words with **k** or **g**. One has been done for you.

1. _ neel

      Answer: *kneel*

2. _ nock

3. _ naw

4. _ nash

5. _ nome

Try these

Look at the groups of words. Write the words and underline the word with the spelling mistake in each group. One has been done for you.

1. know, gnow, now

Answer: know, <u>gnow,</u> now

2. knaw, gnaw, nor

3. knot, gnot, not

4. knew, gnew, new

5. knome, gnome, home

Now try these

Find one or two spelling mistakes in each sentence. Then rewrite the sentences with the correct spelling. Underline the correct spelling. One has been done for you.

1. I now the answer to the question.

Answer: I <u>know</u> the answer to the question.

2. Samir's chest of drawers has blue nobs.

3. The brave night had a sharp nife.

4. A nat bit me on my nee.

5. There is a not in Sam's nitting.

Words beginning with wr–

When a word begins with **wr–**, the **w** is silent and the sound is **/r/**.

- **wr**ite

Get started

Copy and complete the words with **wr–**. One has been done for you.

1. _ _ iter

   Answer: *writer*

2. _ _ote

3. _ _ ench

4. _ _ap

5. _ _eck

6. _ _ inkle

7. _ _ iggle

Try these

Look at the groups of words. Underline the word with the spelling mistake in each group. One has been done for you.

1. wrong, rong, wing

   Answer: *wrong, <u>rong,</u> wing*

2. rest, wrestle, restle

3. riggle, wriggle, wiggle

4. white, write, riting

5. wren, rinkle, weak

Now try these

Find the spelling mistake in each sentence. Then rewrite the sentences with the correct spelling. Underline the correct spelling. One has been done for you.

1. When it is cold, you should rap up well.

   Answer: *When it is cold, you should <u>wrap</u> up well.*

2. My grandma's face is worn and rinkled.

3. Ana hurt her rist when she fell.

4. She ripped off the sweet rapper.

5. Sam restled his brother for the toy.

Words ending in –le

The most common way to spell the **/l/** sound at the end of a word is **–le**.

- tab**le**
- unc**le**
- cyc**le**

Get started

Copy the words and underline **–le**. One has been done for you.

1. cable

Answer: cab<u>le</u>

2. wobble

3. castle

4. simple

5. circle

6. feeble

7. rubble

Try these

Look at the pictures and write the words. One has been done for you.

1.  a _ _ _ _

Answer: *ankle*

2.  t _ _ _ _ _ _ _

3. t _ _ _ _

4.  a _ _ _ _

5.  p _ _ _ _ _

Now try these

Copy and complete the sentences using the words in the box. One has been done for you.

1. The old _____ was in ruins.

Answer: *The old castle was in ruins.*

2. The pain in my foot makes me _____.

3. I have a _____ on top of my hat.

4. My mum told me I was in _____.

5. I love to eat a nice, juicy _____.

> apple
>
> bobble
>
> ~~castle~~
>
> hobble
>
> trouble

Words ending in –el

In some words, the **/l/** sound at the end is spelt **–el**.

- squirr**el**
- kenn**el**
- lev**el**

Get started

Copy the words and underline **–el**. One has been done for you.

1. squirrel

   Answer: squirr<u>el</u>

2. caramel

3. panel

4. towel

5. gravel

6. vowel

7. cancel

Try these

Look at the pairs of words. Copy the word with the correct spelling in each pair. One has been done for you.

1. model, modle

   Answer: *model*

2. parcle, parcel

3. tunnel, tunnell

4. quarrle, quarrel

5. hotel, hotle

Now try these

Copy and complete the sentences using the words in the box. One has been done for you.

1. Riding a scooter is a fun way to _____.

   Answer: *Riding a scooter is a fun way to travel.*

2. Work hard or I will _____ play time.

3. There is a _____ in the queen's crown.

4. I saw a _____ with two humps.

5. Mum used a _____ to wipe my face.

| camel |
| cancel |
| flannel |
| jewel |
| ~~travel~~ |

Words ending in –al

There are some words where the **/l/** sound at the end is spelt **–al**.

- anim**al**
- cere**al**
- classic**al**
- tot**al**

Get started

Copy the words and underline **–al**. One has been done for you.

1. equal

   Answer: equ<u>al</u>

2. admiral

3. canal

4. plural

5. material

Try these

Look at the pictures and write the words. One has been done for you.

1. a_ _ _ _ _   Answer: *animal*

2. s_ _ _ _ _

3.    p_ _ _ _

4. o_ _ _

5. p_ _ _ _

Now try these

Copy and complete the sentences using the words in the box. One has been done for you.

1. Ariella's trumpet is made of _____.

    Answer: *Ariella's trumpet is made of <u>metal</u>.*

2. John Thompson is a very _____ person.

3. We had a great time at the _____.

4. We visited Granny in the _____.

5. The children went through the _____ to a _____ land.

| festival |
| hospital |
| magical |
| ~~metal~~ |
| musical |
| portal |

Words ending in −il

There are some words where the **/l/** sound at the end is spelt **−il**. There are not many of these words.

- pup**il**
- lent**il**

Get started

Copy the words and underline **−il**. One has been done for you.

1. pencil

Answer: penc<u>il</u>

2. peril

3. basil

4. stencil

5. council

6. gerbil

7. until

8. tonsil

Try these

Look at the groups of words. Copy the word with the correct spelling in each group. One has been done for you.

1. pupil, pupal, pupel

    Answer: *pupil*

2. tonsal, tonsel, tonsil

3. evil, evel, eval

4. fossle, fossil, fossel

5. daffodile, daffodle, daffodil

Now try these

Copy and complete the sentences using the words in the box. One has been done for you.

1. I have a pet _____ called Nibbles.

    Answer: *I have a pet gerbil*
             called Nibbles.

2. One day I would like to visit _____.

3. I saw a dinosaur _____ at the museum.

4. I used a _____ to draw a flower.

5. I was not hungry _____ I smelled the chips.

Brazil
fossil
~~gerbil~~
stencil
until

Words ending in –y

The long **/i/** sound at the end of words is often spelt **–y**.

- fl**y**
- b**y**
- sl**y**

Get started

Look at the words in the box. They all end with the long **/i/** sound. Copy the table and write the words in the correct group. One has been done for you.

fly	high	pie	shy	sigh	why	tie

–igh	–ie	–y
		fly

Try these

Put the letters in order to make a correctly spelt word ending in **–y**. One has been done for you.

1. y b

Answer: by

2. y m

3. f y r

4. y k s

Now try these

Copy and complete the sentences using the words in the box. One has been done for you.

1. When Joel woke up, the _____ was blue.

Answer: When Joel woke up, the sky was blue.

2. "Oh, please don't _____," said Raj.

3. Morwenna is a _____, quiet girl.

4. "_____ are you late?" asked the teacher.

5. I like to _____ eggs in the morning.

cry
fry
shy
~~sky~~
why

Review unit 1

Can you remember the spellings you've learned this term?
Answer these questions to find out.

A. Look at the groups of words. Write the word with the
spelling mistake in each group, then write the correct
spelling. One has been done for you.

1. strange, cage, brige

   Answer: ~~brige~~ bridge

2. nice, sity, circle

3. uncel, cycle, table

4. squirrel, towle, wobble

5. rock, wriggle, rong

B. Look at these pictures and write the words.
One has been done for you.

1.  p _ _ _ _ _   Answer: pencil

2.  s q u _ _ _ _ _

3.  c _ _ _ _ _

4.  p _ _ _ _

5.  p _ _ _ _ _

C. Look at the pairs of words. Copy the word with the correct spelling in each pair. One has been done for you.

1. kneel, neel

   Answer: *kneel*

2. nome, gnome

3. fansy, fancy

4. simple, simpel

5. slege, sledge

6. large, lardge

D. Find the spelling mistake in each sentence. Then rewrite the sentences with the correct spelling. Underline the correct spelling. One has been done for you.

1. Snow White heard a nock at the door.

   Answer: *Snow White heard a <u>knock</u> at the door.*

2. Outside there was an old lady selling lase.

3. There was something rong with the old lady.

4. Snow White invited the old lady into the cottige.

5. The old lady gave Snow White a shiny appel.

Adding –es to words ending in –y

When we add **–es** to a word that ends in one consonant followed by **–y**, we change the **y** to **i** and then add **–es**.

- bunny → bunnies
- lily → lilies
- carry → carries

Get started

Look at the words in the box, some end in **–y** and some end in **–es**. Copy the table and write the words in the correct group, putting them in pairs. One has been done for you.

–y	–ies
bunny	bunnies

~~bunny~~
sties
reply
dries
~~bunnies~~
replies
fly
dry
hurry
sty
hurries
flies

Try these

Write the words, changing the **y** to **i** and adding **–es**. One has been done for you.

1. dolly

   Answer: dollies

2. story

3. baby

4. country

5. copy

Now try these

Find the spelling mistake in each sentence. Then rewrite the sentences with the correct spelling. Underline the correct spelling. One has been done for you.

1. Holly has two ponys called Apple and Patch.

   Answer: Holly has two <u>ponies</u> called Apple and Patch.

2. In the end, Cinderella marry Prince Charming.

3. Amy likes counting her penny.

4. In the autumn the trees are full of berry.

5. The baby cry all day and all night.

Adding –ed to words ending in –y

When we add **–ed** to a word that ends in one consonant followed by **–y**, we change the **y** to **i** and then add **–ed**.

- copy → cop**ied**
- bully → bull**ied**
- tidy → tid**ied**

Get started

Look at the words in the box, some end in **–y** and some end in **–ed**. Copy the table and write the words in the correct group, putting them in pairs. One has been done for you.

–y	–ied
worry	worried

~~worry~~	fried
supplied	applied
try	tried
supply	fry
apply	~~worried~~
reply	replied

Try these

Write the words, adding **–ed**. One has been done for you.

1. study

Answer: studied

2. cry

3. spy

4. fancy

5. carry

Now try these

Find the spelling mistake in each sentence. Then rewrite the sentences with the correct spelling. Underline the corrected spelling. One has been done for you.

1. Nia was late so she hurryd to school.

Answer: Nia was late so she <u>hurried</u> to school.

2. I was worrid about the spelling test.

3. I didn't know the answers so I copyed them.

4. I cryd when I watched the sad film.

5. My granddad marrid my granny a long time ago.

Adding –er or –est to root words ending in –y

When we add **–er** or **–est** to a word that ends in one consonant followed by **–y**, we change the **y** to **i** and then add **–er** or **–est**.

- tiny → tini**er** → tini**est**
- fuzzy → fuzzi**er** → fuzzi**est**
- lucky → lucki**er** → lucki**est**

Get started

Look at the pairs of words. Copy the word with the correct spelling in each pair. One has been done for you.

1. happyer, happier

Answer: happier

2. sandyer, sandier

3. merriest, merryest

4. messyer, messiest

5. cosiest, cosyest

Try these

Copy and complete the table. One has been done for you.

1.	pretty	prettier	prettiest
2.	ugly		
3.	lazy		
4.			heaviest
5.		mightier	

Now try these

The underlined words in each sentence are wrong. Rewrite the sentences adding **–er** or **–est** to correct the wrong words. Underline the corrected word. One has been done for you.

1. Princess Navi is the <u>pretty</u> princess in the world.

   Answer: Princess Navi is the <u>prettiest</u> princess in the world.

2. My jokes are <u>funny</u> than yours.

3. I want to be the <u>wealthy</u> person in the world.

4. Kerem is <u>busy</u> than me.

5. Today's test is <u>easy</u> than yesterday's.

Adding –ing to root words ending in –y

When we add **–ing** to a word that ends in **–y**, we just add **–ing**. The root word stays the same.

- fly → fly**ing**
- buy → buy**ing**
- simplify → simplify**ing**

Get started

Copy the words, adding **–ing**. Underline the **–ying** ending. One has been done for you.

1. magnify

Answer:  magnify<u>ing</u>

2. cry

3. try

4. reply

5. apply

Try these

Look at the groups of words. Copy the word with the correct spelling in each group. One has been done for you.

1. carriing, carrying, carrieing

Answer: *carrying*

2. frying, friing, frieing

3. spieing, spiing, spying

4. supplying, supplieing, suppling

5. relying, relieing, reliing

Now try these

Find the wrong word in each sentence. Then rewrite the sentences, adding **–ing** to correct the wrong words. Underline the corrected word. One has been done for you.

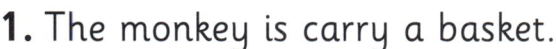

1. The monkey is carry a basket.

Answer: *The monkey is <u>carrying</u> a basket.*

2. The pirates are bury their treasure.

3. Calculators are useful for multiply big numbers.

4. I like looking at ants with my magnify glass.

5. I am try very hard not to cry.

Adding new endings to root words ending in –e

When we add **–ing**, **–ed**, **–er**, **–est** or **–y** to a word that ends in **–e**, we drop the **e** and add the new ending.

- wave → wav**ing** → wav**ed** → wav**y**

- nice → nic**er** → nic**est**

Get started

Look at the pairs of words. Copy the word with the correct spelling in each pair. One has been done for you.

1. waveing, waving

 Answer: *waving*

2. stoney, stony

3. bravest, braveest

4. tradeing, trading

5. exploding, explodeing

Try these

Copy and complete the table. One has been done for you.

		+ –ing	+ –ed
1.	hike	hiking	hiked
2.	blame		
3.	graze		
4.	save		
5.	bake		

Now try these

Find the wrong word in each sentence. Then rewrite the sentences, correcting the wrong words. Underline the corrected word. One has been done for you.

1. When I hear a good joke, I can't help smile.

   Answer: When I hear a good joke, I can't help <u>smiling</u>.

2. The air gets very smoke when we light fires.

3. At last we escape from the dragon.

4. Yesterday, we dance all afternoon.

5. My dog is always chase rabbits.

Adding new endings to one-syllable words with short vowel sounds

When we add **–ing**, **–ed**, **–er**, **–est** or **–y** to a word that ends with a short vowel followed by a single consonant, we usually double the consonant before adding the new ending.

- run → runn**ing** → runn**er** → runn**y**

- slim → slimm**er** → slimm**est**

Get started

Write the words, adding the endings. Underline the double consonant. One has been done for you.

1. run + –ing

   Answer: ru<u>nn</u>ing

2. slam + –ed

3. thin + –er

4. flat + –est

5. nut + –y

Try these

Copy and complete the table. One has been done for you.

		+ –er	+ –est
1.	slim	slimmer	slimmest
2.	thin		
3.	fit		
4.	sad		
5.	fat		

Now try these

Find the wrong word in each sentence. Then rewrite the sentences, correcting the wrong words. Underline the corrected words. One has been done for you.

1. The woman is pet the cat.

    Answer: The woman is <u>petting</u> the cat.

2. My brother cried when he pop his balloon.

3. Dad and I went shop after school.

4. We are having a picnic because it is a sun day.

5. The book was so fun that I laughed out loud.

Spelling words with al or all

The long vowel sound **/or/** is usually spelt **a** before **l** or **ll**.

- c**all**
- w**a**lk
- hold**all**

Get started

Look at the words in the box. Sort the words into words with /or/ spelt **al** and words with /or/ spelt **all**. Copy the table and write the words in the correct group. One has been done for you.

al	all
	ball

```
ball
fall
hall
stalk
stall
talk
```

Try these

Complete the words with **al** or **all**. One has been done for you.

1. c _ _ _

    Answer: call

2. b _ _ d

3. _ _ so

4. t _ _ _

5. w _ _ k

Now try these

Copy and complete the sentences with the words in the box. One has been done for you.

1. Giraffes are very _____.

    Answer: Giraffes are very tall.

2. Mice are very _____ .

3. I _____ do my homework on time.

4. Humpty Dumpty fell off the _____.

5. I love carrot and _____ cake.

always
small
~~tall~~
wall
walnut

The /u/ sound spelt o

In some words the short vowel sound **/u/** is spelt **o**.

- s**o**n

- c**o**ver

- n**o**ne

Get started

Copy the words and underline the **/u/** sound. One has been done for you.

1. brother

   Answer: br<u>o</u>ther

2. mother

3. nothing

4. Monday

5. worry

6. another

7. glove

8. month

Try these

Look at the groups of words. Copy the word with the correct spelling in each group. One has been done for you.

1. month, munth, manth

Answer: *month*

2. uther, other, outher

3. wurry, wurrie, worry

4. nothing, nuthing, nuffing

5. bruther, bruver, brother

Now try these

Find the wrong word in each sentence. Then rewrite the sentences, correcting the wrong words. Underline the corrected words. One has been done for you.

1. The muther cat has three kittens.

Answer: *The <u>mother</u> cat has three kittens.*

2. I threw a snowball at my bruther.

3. I wurry a lot about spelling tests.

4. Nuthing is tastier than chocolate cake.

5. Billy's mum is very proud of her sun.

The /ee/ sound spelt –ey

Read these words: key, donkey, monkey

What sound can you hear at the end? That's right – an **/ee/** sound. The **/ee/** sound is spelt **ey**.

When we add **s** to words that end **–ey**, the ending does not change – we just add the **s**. Simple! Look at these words:

- one key → two key**s**
- one donkey → two donkey**s**

Get started

Look at the groups of words. Copy the word with the correct spelling in each group. One has been done for you.

1. monkeys, monkies, monkees

   Answer: monkeys

2. chutnees, chutnies, chutneys

3. journeys, journies, journees

4. trollees, trolleys, trollies

5. vallees, valleys, vallies

Try these

Put the letters in order to create one of the words in the box. One has been done for you.

keys
~~turkeys~~
pulleys
chimneys
donkeys

1. kyurtes

   Answer: *turkeys*

2. kdeonsy

3. echiymn

4. seyllup

5. ekys

Now try these

Find the wrong word in each sentence. Then rewrite the sentences, correcting the wrong words. Underline the corrected words. One has been done for you.

1. There were three donkey in the field.

   Answer: *There were three <u>donkeys</u> in the field.*

2. Smoke was coming out of all the chimney.

3. The city has lots of dark, twisting alley.

4. The gatekeeper carried a big bunch of key.

5. The jockey are all trying to win the race.

The /o/ sound spelt a after w and qu

In many words the vowel sound **/o/** is spelt **a** after **w** or **qu**.

- sw**a**n

- w**a**nt

- qu**a**ntity

Get started

Copy the words and underline the **/o/** sound. One has been done for you.

1. swan

   Answer: sw<u>a</u>n

2. squash

3. swamp

4. quality

5. was

Try these

Look at the pictures and write the words. One has been done for you.

 1. w_ _ _

Answer: wasp

 2. w_ _ _

 3. s_ _ _

 4. w_ _ _ _

Now try these

Find the spelling mistake in each sentence. Then rewrite the sentences with the correct spelling. Underline the correct spelling. One has been done for you.

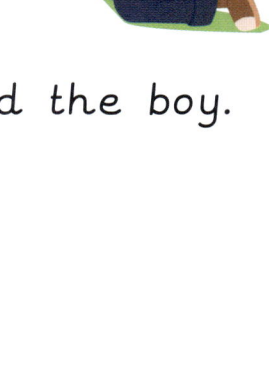

1. "I wont a hamster!" said the boy.

   Answer: "I <u>want</u> a hamster!" said the boy.

2. Chen looked at his wotch to see the time.

3. Please could I swop places with you?

4. Don't forget to wosh your hands.

5. Swollow your food before you speak.

The /er/ sound spelt or after w

In some words the **/er/** sound is spelt **or** after **w**.

- w**or**ld

- w**or**se

- crossw**or**d

Get started

Look at the words in the box. Copy the words with the **/er/** sound. One has been done for you.

~~work~~	short	oral
fort	silkworm	worst
north	sword	worm
worth	worn	world

Answer: work

Try these

Put the letters in order to make a correctly spelt word from the box. One has been done for you.

working	workshop	~~world~~	worm	worthy

1. owldr

Answer: *world*

2. wronkig

3. tworhy

4. mrow

5. rowskhop

Now try these

Find the spelling mistake in each sentence. Then rewrite the sentences with the correct spelling. Underline the correct spelling. One has been done for you.

1. Birds think earthwerms are a tasty treat.

Answer: Birds think <u>earthworms</u> are a tasty treat.

2. Churches, temples and mosques are places of wership.

3. Wirkmen are digging up the road again.

4. Today has been the wurst day ever!

5. I helped Granddad in his werkshop today.

Review unit 2

Can you remember the spellings you've learned this term? Answer these questions to find out.

A. Look at these pictures and write the words. One has been done for you.

1.  t _ _ _ _ _

    Answer: *turkey*

2. b _ _ _ _ _ _

3. 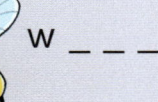 w _ _ _

4. b _ _ _

5. p _ _ _ _ _

6. m _ _ _ _ _

B. Write the words, adding the endings. Remember, you might need to change some letters. One has been done for you.

1. hurry + –es

    Answer: *hurries*

2. baby + –es

3. copy + –ing

4. flat + –er

5. lucky + –est

6. run + –ing

7. joke + –er

8. cold + –est

C. Look at the pairs of words. Copy the word with the correct spelling in each pair. One has been done for you.

1. Monday, Munday

   Answer: Monday

2. sky, skigh

3. bruvver, brother

4. squash, squosh

5. allee, alley

6. watch, woch

D. Find the spelling mistake in each sentence. Then rewrite the sentences with the correct spelling. Underline the correct spelling. One has been done for you.

1. Pushkal dropped the glass he was carriing.

   Answer: Pushkal dropped the glass he was <u>carrying</u>.

2. My dress was the fancyest at the party.

3. Only three boys replyed to my invitation.

4. Five swons swam past me.

5. You must wear your gluvs to play in the snow.

The /or/ sound spelt ar after w

In many words the **/or/** sound is spelt **ar** after **w**.

- w**ar**m

- w**ar**

- aw**ar**d

Get started

Look at the words in the box. Copy the words with the **/or/** sound. One has been done for you.

~~warm~~	guard	wart
charm	swarm	yarn
warp	ward	war
farm	sparkle	dark

Answer: warm

Try these

Put the letters in order to create one of the words in the box. One has been done for you.

wardrobe	dwarf	warmth	award	~~warble~~

1. arbewl

   Answer: warble

2. radaw

3. wfrad

4. ardbreow

5. thramw

Now try these

Find the spelling mistake in each sentence. Then rewrite the sentences with the correct spelling. Underline the correct spelling. One has been done for you.

1. The sky was blue and the sun was worm.

   Answer: The sky was blue and the sun was <u>warm</u>.

2. Kamla worned us that the food was hot.

3. I won an aword for all my hard work.

4. Dan's a wanted man: there's a reword for his arrest.

5. The world should make peace, not wor.

The /zh/ sound spelt s

When there is a buzzing sound in the middle of a word, it is sometimes spelt **s**.

- televi**s**ion
- trea**s**ure
- clo**s**ure

Get started

Copy the words and underline the **s** that stands for a buzzing sound. One has been done for you.

1. television

   Answer: televi_s_ion

2. vision

3. measure

4. division

5. erosion

6. treasure

7. usual

Try these

Look at the words in the box. In some words there is a **/sh/** sound spelt **sh** and in other words there is a **/zh/** sound spelt **s**. Copy the table and write the words in the correct group. One has been done for you.

~~decision~~	measure	mushroom
fishing	cushion	usual

/zh/ spelt **s**	**/sh/** spelt **sh**
decision	

Now try these

Find the spelling mistake in each sentence. Then rewrite the sentences with the correct spelling. Underline the correct spelling. One has been done for you.

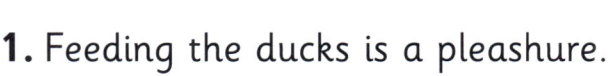

1. Feeding the ducks is a pleashure.

   Answer: Feeding the ducks is a <u>pleasure</u>.

2. The pirates are following a treazure map.

3. I like to watch televishion in the morning.

4. Suddenly there was an incredible exploshion.

5. It was unushual for Hassan to be late.

Adding the suffixes –ment, –ness, –ful, –less and –ly (1)

Most root words form new words with the suffixes **–ment**, **–ness**, **–ful**, **–less** and **–ly** without adding, dropping or changing letters.

- enjoy + –ment → enjoyment
- tired + –ness → tiredness
- use + –ful → useful
- help + –less → helpless
- brilliant + –ly → brilliantly

Get started

Write the words, adding the suffixes. One has been done for you.

1. tired + –ness

    Answer: *tiredness*

2. plain + –ly

3. entertain + –ment

4. play + –ful

5. heart + –less

Try these

Match the words with suffixes to their root words. One has been done for you.

1. sweetness

2. fulfilment

3. thankless

4. shameful

a) thank

b) shame

c) sweet

d) fulfil

Now try these

Choose a suffix from the box to correct the underlined word in each sentence. Write the sentence with the correct word. One has been done for you.

less	~~ness~~	ful	ly

1. Tortoises are known for their slow.

Answer: *Tortoises are known for their <u>slowness</u>.*

2. The kittens are <u>play</u> little things.

3. "This is stupid," said Thomas <u>cross</u>.

4. The duke is a cruel and <u>heart</u> man.

Adding the suffixes –ment, –ness, –ful, –less and –ly (2)

Most root words form new words with the suffixes **–ment**, **–ness**, **–ful**, **–less** and **–ly** without adding, dropping or changing letters.

- quick + –ly → quickly

But if the root word is two syllables long and ends in one consonant and **–y**, we change the **y** to **i** and then add the suffix.

- easy + –ly → easily
- happy + –ness → happiness

Get started

Look at the words in the box. Some words have one syllable and other words have two syllables. Copy the table and write the words in the correct group. One has been done for you.

One syllable	Two syllables
	angry

angry
dry
happy
lucky
sly
soppy

Try these

Write the words, adding suffixes and making any necessary changes to the spelling of the root word. One has been done for you.

1. happy + –ness

    Answer: *happiness*

2. soppy + –ness

3. sly + –ly

4. lucky + –ly

5. angry + –ly

6. dry + –ness

Now try these

The underlined words in each sentence are wrong. Rewrite the sentences, adding **–ly** to correct the wrong words. Underline the corrected words. One has been done for you.

1. The school band played <u>noisy</u>.

    Answer: *The school band played <u>noisily</u>.*

2. <u>Bright</u> coloured butterflies flew by.

3. It was raining but <u>lucky</u> I had my umbrella.

4. Annabelle stretched and yawned <u>sleepy</u>.

5. <u>Amazing</u>, no one was hurt in the accident.

Apostrophes for contractions

Sometimes we shorten a word by leaving out one or more letters. We use an **apostrophe** (') in place of the letter or letters and we join the shortened word to the word before it. We write the two words as one word. Words like this are called **contractions**.

- did not → didn't

- she has → she's

- you had better → you'd better

Get started

Match the full words to the contractions. One has been done for you.

1. I am   **a)** hasn't

2. could not   **b)** I'm

3. has not   **c)** there's

4. she will   **d)** couldn't

5. there is   **e)** she'll

Try these

Write the contractions as full words. One has been done for you.

1. he's got

Answer: he has got

2. I'll

3. don't

4. they've

5. wasn't

Now try these

Rewrite the sentences using contractions for the underlined words. One has been done for you.

1. "<u>I will</u> take the dog for a walk," said Dad.

Answer: "I'll take the dog for a walk," said Dad.

2. "<u>What is</u> the problem?" asked Mum.

3. "<u>That is</u> enough!" shouted Mrs Jones.

4. "<u>I am</u> not feeling very well," said Daisy.

5. "<u>Does not</u> that work?" asked Riz.

Apostrophes to show possession

To show **possession**, in other words, to show that something belongs to someone, we add an **apostrophe** and an **s** to the word.

- Harri**'s** scooter
- the chair**'s** seat

Get started

Copy the phrases and underline the apostrophe and **s**. One has been done for you.

1. Jorge's parents

   Answer: Jorge<u>'s</u> parents

2. the chicken's eggs
3. the children's homework
4. the book's cover
5. Meghan's bag

Try these

Copy the table and write the phrases in the correct group. Add the apostrophe where it is needed. One has been done for you.

~~Sandeeps bike~~	the horses in the field
tables and chairs	the new gym kits
the cars wheels	the suns rays

Phrases with apostrophe	Phrases without apostrophe
Sandeep's bike	

Now try these

Copy the sentences adding the missing apostrophes. One has been done for you.

1. The monkeys tail is very long.

   Answer: The monkey's tail is very long.

2. The rabbits floppy ears are very soft.

3. The coats buttons are coming off.

4. Those are Haritas shoes and gloves.

5. Franks socks are just like mine.

Words ending in –tion

The **/shun/** sound at the ends of some words is spelt **–tion**.

- educa**tion**
- na**tion**
- condi**tion**

Get started

Copy and complete the words with **–tion**. One has been done for you.

1. educa _ _ _ _

   Answer: education

2. ac _ _ _ _

3. collec _ _ _ _

4. por _ _ _ _

5. sec _ _ _ _

6. competi _ _ _ _

7. defini _ _ _ _

Try these

Look at the groups of words. Copy the word with the correct spelling in each group. One has been done for you.

1. station, stashun, stasion

   Answer: *station*

2. secsion, section, secshun

3. posision, posishon, position

4. question, queschion, queston

5. mocion, motion, moshion

Now try these

Copy and complete the sentences with the words in the box. One has been done for you.

directions	~~fiction~~	option	pollution	solution

1. I love science _____ stories.

   Answer: *I love science fiction stories.*

2. My friend gave me _____ to his house.

3. The factory chimneys filled the air with _____.

4. I'm sure we can find a _____ to the problem.

5. Meg chose the vegetarian _____.

Homophones (1)

Some words sound the same but they are not spelt the same and they do not mean the same. We call these words **homophones**.

- **right** (adjective) and **write** (verb)
- **meet** (verb) and **meat** (noun)

Get started

Match the homophones. One has been done for you.

1. right   **a)** so

2. sew   **b)** write

3. hear   **c)** their

4. there   **d)** hole

5. whole   **e)** here

Try these

Copy and complete the sentences with one of the homophones in brackets. One has been done for you.

1. Please come _____. (here / hear)

Answer: *Please come <u>here</u>.*

2. They are putting on _____ shoes. (there / their)

3. I want the _____ class to listen to me. (whole / hole)

4. That is the _____ answer. (right / write)

Now try these

Copy and complete the sentences using some of the words in the box. One has been done for you.

hear	~~hole~~	sew	their	they're	write
here	right	so	there	whole	

1. There's a _____ in my bag.

Answer: *There's a <u>hole</u> in my bag.*

2. Can you _____ the music?

3. I am going to _____ a letter to my friend.

4. I need to _____ the hole in my trousers.

5. _____ staying at _____ granny's house.

Homophones and near homophones

Some words sound the same or nearly the same but they are not spelt the same and they do not mean the same. We call these words **homophones** or **near homophones**.

- homophones: **bear** (noun) and **bare** (adjective)

- near homophones: **poor** (adj) and **pour** (verb)

Get started

Match the homophones. One has been done for you.

1. *bear*   **a)** quiet

2. pear   **b)** *bare*

3. blew   **c)** pair

4. sea   **d)** see

5. quite   **e)** blue

Try these

Copy and complete the sentences with one of the homophones in brackets. One has been done for you.

1. I have a cuddly teddy _____. (bear / bare)

   Answer: *I have a cuddly teddy bear.*

2. The juicy _____ was delicious. (pair / pear)

3. The _____ is blue today. (see / sea)

4. It is _____ in the library. (quite / quiet)

5. I am _____ good at playing the piano. (quite / quiet)

Now try these

Copy and complete the sentences with some of the words in the box. One has been done for you.

bare	blew	~~pair~~	quiet	sea
bear	blue	pear	quite	see

1. I have a new _____ of shoes.

   Answer: *I have a new pair of shoes.*

2. Can you _____ the bus coming?

3. I _____ out the candles on my birthday cake.

4. I am _____ sure that I am right.

5. He walked on the sand with _____ feet.

Homophones (2)

Some words sound the same but they are not spelt the same and they do not mean the same. We call these words **homophones**.

- A **knight** is a man who fights for his king or queen.

- **Night** is a time of darkness between sunrise and sunset.

Get started

Match the homophones. One has been done for you.

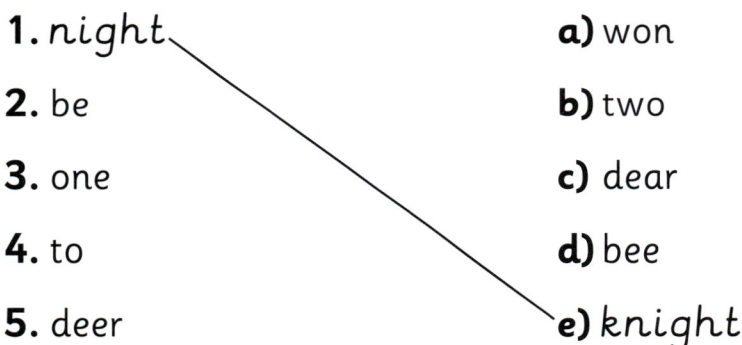

1. night

2. be

3. one

4. to

5. deer

a) won

b) two

c) dear

d) bee

e) knight

Which of these homophones are numbers? Write the words.

Try these

Copy and complete the sentences with one of the homophones in brackets. One has been done for you.

1. It is good to _____ kind to others. (be / bee)

   Answer: It is good to <u>be</u> kind to others.

2. The _____ buzzed near my nose. (be / bee)

3. Mum says I eat _____ many sweets. (too / two)

4. The moon shines at _____. (knight / night)

5. It is time for us to go _____ bed. (to / too / two)

Now try these

Copy and complete the sentences using some of the words in the box. One has been done for you.

be	knight	~~one~~	to	two
bee	night	won	too	

1. I have two cakes. Would you like _____?

   Answer: I have two cakes. Would you like <u>one</u>?

2. I was happy when my team _____ the cup.

3. The _____ put on his armour.

4. I went to the park. Jane came _____.

5. I have _____ sisters and a brother.

Review unit 3

Can you remember the spellings you've learned this term?
Answer these questions to find out.

A. Look at the groups of words. Write the word with the spelling mistake in each group, then write the correct spelling. One has been done for you.

1. work, worm, wor

    Answer: ~~wor~~ *war*

2. world, werst, warm

3. television, treasure, uzual

4. meazure, division, vision

5. really, easilly, kindly

B. Write the words, adding the endings. Remember, you might need to change some letters. One has been done for you.

1. noise + –ly

    Answer: *noisily*

2. move + –ment

3. happy + –ness

4. easy + –ly

5. harm + –less

C. Write these phrases using contractions. One has been done for you.

1. I am

    Answer: *I'm*

2. was not

3. she is

4. they will

5. we will

D. These phrases each have a missing apostrophe. Write out the phrases putting in the missing apostrophes. One has been done for you.

1. Janas coming to tea.

   Answer: <u>Jana's</u> coming to tea.

2. Theres my bag!

3. Find Chloes shoes.

4. This chairs legs are wobbly.

E. Copy and complete the sentences with the correct spelling from the brackets. One has been done for you.

1. Please _____ me a cup of tea.
   (pour / poor)

   Answer: Please <u>pour</u> me a cup of tea.

2. Can you _____ me talking to you?
   (here / hear)

3. Hooray – _____ coming now!
   (their / they're)

4. My train arrives at the _____ at 2 o'clock.
   (station / stashon)

5. The _____ say we should go left here.
   (direcsions / directions)